SCHOLASTIC

W9-APR-845

Building Vocabulary With Familiar Songs

A Unique and Fun Way to Motivate Students to Play With Language and Enrich Their Vocabulary

by Kathleen Dorsey

New York • Toronto • London • Auckland • Sydney
Mexico City • New Delhi • Hong Kong • Buenos Aires

Teaching *Resources*

Cover design by Jason Robinson
Interior design by NEO Grafika Studio Inc.
Illustrations by Mike Moran

ISBN-13: 978-0-439-81311-2
ISBN-10: 0-439-81311-5
Copyright © 2007 by Kathleen Dorsey
All rights reserved.
Printed in the U.S.A.

1 2 3 4 5 6 7 8 9 10   40   15 14 13 12 11 10 09 08 07

Table of Contents

Introduction

Vocabulary is an interesting issue. Much has been written and designed to help improve phonemic awareness, decoding skills, fluency, and comprehension. However, as a teacher, I have noticed through the years that even when students are fluently decoding words at an acceptable rate, they are unable to "comprehend" the paragraph, story, or passage read.

Upon investigation and discussions with students it became apparent that what's missing is an understanding of the vocabulary. While students may be able to accurately decode a word, they may never have encountered it before or may have no idea what it means.

Building Vocabulary With Familiar Songs is designed to supplement your current vocabulary instruction with a technique that is engaging and motivating for all students. It introduces students to and familiarizes them with new words and their meanings through the use of well-known songs and rhymes. The exercise is a simple one: Students start by singing or reciting a familiar song or rhyme and discuss what it means. Over the next few days, you replace some of the lyrics with synonyms from a word bank and invite students to sing the revised song with the new words. By practicing the song repeatedly on a daily basis, students get multiple encounters with the new words, helping them retain the words and their meanings. This technique can be used for any age, but I targeted Grades 3 to 6 because that is when I feel students really need to increase their vocabulary to understand the texts that they read.

What Research Says About Vocabulary Learning

There are many ways to teach vocabulary. Research indicates that vocabulary knowledge can be acquired both through the context in which words are used (Nagy, Herman, & Anderson, 1985) and through direct instruction (McKeown & Beck, 1988). Based on how an unfamiliar word is used in a sentence or passage, readers could infer what the word means. Researchers estimate that readers can learn between 5 and 15 percent of unfamiliar words through context (Nagy et al., 1985; Swanborn & de Glopper, 1999). Other words can be learned through direct instruction. This doesn't mean teaching students how to look up words in a dictionary. Rather, direct instruction encourages students to actively think about words and their meanings and to use them in appropriate ways. Beck and associates recommend teaching students "Tier 2 words"—words that appear frequently in a wide variety of texts and in the written and oral language of mature language users. (Tier 1 words are basic words, such as *clock*, *boy*, and *run*. Tier 3 words are more specialized and have narrow use, such as *isotope* and *isthmus*.) (Beck, McKeown, & Kucan, 2002). Well-known children's songs provide a familiar context through which students can acquire and retain the meaning of new, Tier 2 words—the synonyms used in place of the regular lyrics. Christen and Murphy's research (1991) shows the integration of new information with information that is already known is helpful for vocabulary acquisition.

How to Use This Book

Select a song or rhyme from the book. Copy the page(s) on a transparency to display on an overhead projector or write it on chart paper. You may also want to make photocopies of the song or rhyme and distribute to students. Invite students to sing or recite the song or rhyme, then discuss what it means. This part of the activity could take one or two days for about five to ten minutes a day, depending on how well students know the song/rhyme. (This makes a good beginning or end-of-the-day activity.)

When you have determined that students are familiar with the original song/rhyme, it's time to introduce it using synonyms. Copy the activity sheet(s) on a transparency (or write it on chart paper) and make photocopies for students. As a class, fill in the blanks with synonyms from the word bank. Most missing words will have more than one synonym. Choose one synonym to use for each word. Encourage students to write the new words on their sheets. Then invite the class to sing or recite the song/rhyme again, this time with the replacement words. Have the class sing or recite the song/rhyme with the new words over the next two days for about five to ten minutes per day. This will help them retain the words. On the following days, replace the words with another set of synonyms and repeat the process, having students practice the new words for two days.

This can be done up to ten days, using only five to ten minutes per day. Depending on the song or rhyme, students can learn 10 to 20 new vocabulary words in this time period. The technique is based on two things: knowledge of synonyms and short practices repeated daily. When I first experimented with this technique, I conducted a vocabulary test before introducing the activity. Students knew an average of about four out of the 13 to 18 new words used in the pretest. Following about 12 days of practice, students knew an average of 12 to 14 words—an increase of about eight words.

Students find this method enjoyable because of the use of music and because they are already so familiar with the songs and rhymes being used. The music and rhymes appeal to a variety of learners. Auditory learners enjoy the recitation. Visual learners use the text. Kinesthetic learners can act out the songs. Artistic learners can draw pictures to enhance the meanings of the words.

How to Extend the Concept

While the concept is essentially a simple one, there are many ways you can expand upon it:

- Students can work in small groups and use a thesaurus to find their own synonyms for songs or rhymes of their choice. They can then teach the new words to the class. Wilkinson (1996) suggests combining both cooperative learning and story development to make vocabulary learning more exciting.

- Artistic students can create posters about the songs, incorporating pictures for words.

- Students can identify new vocabulary as they read in other areas or in their novels. As students come across interesting words in their reading or dictionary work, they can find a song or rhyme where that word would work.

Comprehending what they read is vitally important to students' success. This book offers a fun and engaging way to introduce new vocabulary without taking up large amounts of valuable teaching time.

Be Kind to Your Web-Footed Friends

Be kind to your web-footed friends,
For a duck may be somebody's mother.
Be kind to your friends in the swamp,
Where the weather is always damp.
You may think that this is the end.
Well, it is!

Name _____   Date _____

Be Kind to Your Web-Footed Friends

Word Bank

acquaintances   believe   compassionate   clammy   comrades

bog   imagine   moist   marsh   conclusion   considerate

finale   benevolent

climate   morass   associates   humid   assume

Directions: Fill in the blanks with synonyms from the Word Bank.

Be _____ to your web-footed _____,
     kind   friends

For a duck may be somebody's mother.

Be _____ to your _____ in the
     kind   friends

_____,
    swamp

Where the _____ is always _____.
             weather   damp

You may _____ that this is the _____.
           think   end

Well, it is!

In a Cabin in the Woods

In a cabin in the woods
Little old man by the window stood,
Saw a rabbit hopping by,
Knocking at his door.

"Help me, help me, help," he said,
"Or the hunter will shoot me dead."
"Little rabbit, come inside.
 Safely to abide."

Building Vocabulary With Familiar Songs © 2007 by Kathleen Dorsey, Scholastic Teaching Resources

Name _____   Date _____

In a Cabin in the Woods

cottage

bounding

observed

assist

bungalow

lodge

elderly

begged

miniature

dwell

watched

skipping

petite

tapping

securely

mature

thumping

rapping

diminutive

reside

aid

pleaded

entrance

Directions: Fill in the blanks with synonyms from the Word Bank.

In a _____ in the woods
  cabin

_____ _____ man by
  Little   old

the window stood,

_____ a rabbit _____ by,
  Saw   hopping

_____ at his _____.
  Knocking   door

"_____ me, _____ me,
  Help   help

_____" he _____,
  help   said

"Or the hunter will shoot me dead."

"_____ rabbit, come inside.
  Little

_____ to _____."
  Safely   abide

Do Your Ears Hang Low?

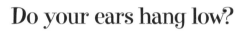

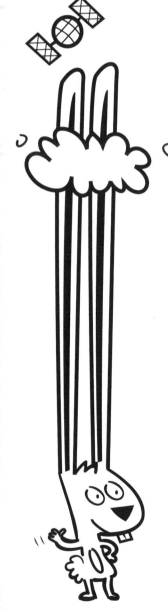
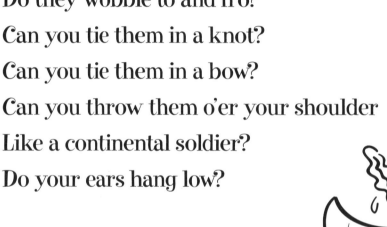

Do your ears hang low?
Do they wobble to and fro?
Can you tie them in a knot?
Can you tie them in a bow?
Can you throw them o'er your shoulder
Like a continental soldier?
Do your ears hang low?

Do your ears hang high?
Do they reach up to the sky?
Do they wrinkle when they're wet?
Do they straighten when they're dry?
Can you wave them at your neighbor
With an element of flavor?
Do your ears hang high?

Do your ears hang wide?

Do they flap from side to side?

Do they wave in the breeze

From the slightest little sneeze?

Can you soar above the nation

With a feeling of elation?

Do your ears hang wide?

Do your ears fall off

When you give a great big cough?

Do they lie there on the ground

Or bounce up at every sound?

Can you stick them in your pocket

Just like Davy Crocket?

Do your ears fall off?

Name _____   Date _____

 # Do Your Ears Hang Low?

Word Bank

dangle

desiccated

droop

country

dehydrated

bind

realm

moist

drape

fling

vibrate

undulate

crumple

rumple

atmosphere

brandish

sodden

crease

soppy

firmament

quiver

fasten

tremble

parched

Directions: Fill in the blanks with synonyms from the Word Bank.

Do your ears _____ low?
_{hang}

Do they _____ to and fro?
_{wobble}

Can you _____ them in a knot?
_{tie}

Can you _____ them in a bow?
_{tie}

Can you _____ them o'er your shoulder
_{throw}

Like a continental soldier?

Do your ears _____ low?
_{hang}

Do your ears hang high?

Do they reach up to the _____?
_{sky}

Do they _____ when they're _____?
_{wrinkle}   _{wet}

Do they straighten when they're _____?
_{dry}

Can you _____ them at your neighbor
_{wave}

With an element of flavor?

Do your ears hang high?

Building Vocabulary With Familiar Songs © 2007 by Kathleen Dorsey, Scholastic Teaching Resources

Do your ears hang wide?

Do they _____ from side to side?
flap

Do they _____ in the _____
wave   breeze

From the slightest _____ sneeze?
little

Can you _____ above the _____
soar   nation

With a _____ of elation?
feeling

Do your ears hang wide?

Do your ears fall off

When you give a great _____ cough?
big

Do they _____ there on the ground
lie

Or _____ up at every _____?
bounce   sound

Can you _____ them in your pocket
stick

Just like Davy Crocket?

Do your ears fall off?

pitch

miniature

minute

resonance

deposit

gust

gigantic

plunk

rebound

sensation

draft

homeland

escalate

ascend

reverberation

spring

enormous

flutter

recline

immense

flail

Itsy Bitsy Spider

The itsy bitsy spider
Climbed up the waterspout.
Down came the rain
And washed the spider out.
Out came the sun
And dried up all the rain,
And the itsy bitsy spider
Climbed up the spout again.

ItSy Bitsy Spider

Word Bank

diminutive   drizzle   clambered   ascended   mounted

swept   precipitation   minute   evaporated

arachnid   scaled   minuscule   inundated

Directions: Fill in the blanks with synonyms from the Word Bank.

The _____   _____
          itsy bitsy   spider

_____ up the waterspout.
       Climbed

Down came the _____
                              rain

And _____ the _____ out.
          washed   spider

Out came the sun and _____ all the rain,
                                    dried up

And the _____   _____
                  itsy bitsy   spider

_____ up the spout again.
       Climbed

The Farmer in the Dell

The farmer in the dell
The farmer in the dell
Hi-ho, the derry-o
The farmer in the dell

The farmer takes a wife
The farmer takes a wife
Hi-ho, the derry-o
The farmer takes a wife

The wife takes a child
The wife takes a child
Hi-ho, the derry-o
The wife takes a child

The child takes a nurse
The child takes a nurse
Hi-ho, the derry-o
The child takes a nurse

The nurse takes a cow
The nurse takes a cow
Hi-ho, the derry-o
The nurse takes a cow

The cow takes a dog
The cow takes a dog
Hi-ho, the derry-o
The cow takes a dog

The dog takes a cat
The dog takes a cat
Hi-ho, the derry-o
The dog takes a cat

The cat takes a rat
The cat takes a rat
Hi-ho, the derry-o
The cat takes a rat

The rat takes the cheese
The rat takes the cheese
Hi-ho, the derry-o
The rat takes the cheese

The cheese stands alone
The cheese stands alone
Hi-ho, the derry-o
The cheese stands alone

The Farmer in the Dell

Word Bank

Directions: Fill in the blanks with synonyms from the Word Bank.

spouse

hollow

descendant

obtains

procures

nanny

acquires

offspring

baby-sitter

The farmer in the _____
                              dell

The farmer in the _____
                              dell

Hi-ho, the derry-o

The farmer in the _____
                              dell

The farmer _____ a _____
                  takes   wife

The farmer _____ a _____
                  takes   wife

Hi-ho, the derry-o

The farmer _____ a _____
                  takes   wife

The wife _____ a _____
                takes   child

The wife _____ a _____
                takes   child

Hi-ho, the derry-o

The wife _____ a _____
                takes   child

The child _____ a _____
                 takes   nurse

The child _____ a _____
                 takes   nurse

Hi-ho, the derry-o

The child _____ a _____
                 takes   nurse

The nurse _____ a _____
                 takes   cow

The nurse _____ a _____

Hi-ho, the derry-o

The nurse _____takes_____ a _____cow_____

The cow _____takes_____ a _____dog_____

The cow _____takes_____ a _____dog_____

Hi-ho, the derry-o

The cow _____takes_____ a _____dog_____

The dog _____takes_____ a _____cat_____

The dog _____takes_____ a _____cat_____

Hi-ho, the derry-o

The dog _____takes_____ a _____cat_____

The cat _____takes_____ a _____rat_____

The cat _____takes_____ a _____rat_____

Hi-ho, the derry-o

The cat _____takes_____ a _____rat_____

The rat _____takes_____ the cheese

The rat _____takes_____ the cheese

Hi-ho, the derry-o

The rat _____takes_____ the cheese

The cheese _____stands_____ _____alone_____

The cheese _____stands_____ _____alone_____

Hi-ho, the derry-o

The cheese _____stands_____ _____alone_____

Five Little Monkeys

Five little monkeys jumping on the bed.
One fell off and bumped his head.
So Momma called the doctor and the doctor said,
"No more monkeys jumping on the bed!"

Four little monkeys jumping on the bed.
One fell off and bumped his head.
So Momma called the doctor and the doctor said,
"No more monkeys jumping on the bed!"

Three little monkeys jumping on the bed.
One fell off and bumped his head.
So Momma called the doctor and the doctor said,
"No more monkeys jumping on the bed!"

Two little monkeys jumping on the bed.
One fell off and bumped her head.
So Momma called the doctor and the doctor said,
"No more monkeys jumping on the bed!"

One little monkey jumping on the bed.
He fell off and bumped his head.
So Momma called the doctor and the doctor said,
"No more monkeys jumping on the bed!"

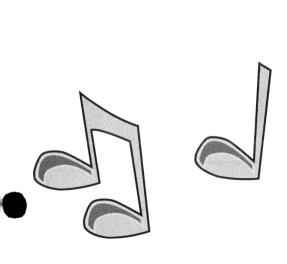

Name _____   Date _____

Five Little Monkeys

Word Bank

Directions: Fill in the blanks with synonyms from the Word Bank.

medic

diminutive

smacked

physician

walloped

leaping

instructed

summoned

cranium

ordered

vaulting

Five _____ _____
little   monkeys

_____ on the bed.
jumping

One _____ off and _____ his
fell   bumped

_____.
head

So Momma _____ the _____ and the
called   doctor

_____ _____,
doctor   said

"No more _____ _____ on the bed!"
monkeys   jumping

Four _____ _____
little   monkeys

_____ on the bed.
jumping

One _____ off and _____ his
fell   bumped

_____.
head

So Momma _____ the _____ and the
called   doctor

_____ _____,
doctor   said

"No more _____ _____ on the bed!"
monkeys   jumping

Three _____ _____
little   monkeys

_____ on the bed.
jumping

One _____ off and _____ his
　　　　fell　　　　　　　　　　　　bumped

_____ .
　head

So Momma _____ the _____ and the
　　　　　　　called　　　　　　　　　　doctor

_____ _____ ,
　doctor　　　　　　　said

"No more _____ _____ on the bed!"
　　　　　monkeys　　　　　　jumping

Two _____ _____
　　　little　　　　　　　monkeys

_____ on the bed.
　jumping

One _____ off and _____ her
　　　fell　　　　　　　　　　　　bumped

_____ .
　head

So Momma _____ the _____ and the
　　　　　　　called　　　　　　　　　　doctor

_____ _____ ,
　doctor　　　　　　　said

"No more _____ _____ on the bed!"
　　　　　monkeys　　　　　　jumping

One _____ _____
　　　little　　　　　　　monkey

_____ on the bed.
　jumping

He _____ off and _____ his
　　fell　　　　　　　　　　　　bumped

_____ .
　head

So Momma _____ the _____ and the
　　　　　　　called　　　　　　　　　　doctor

_____ _____ ,
　doctor　　　　　　　said

"No more _____ _____ on the bed!"
　　　　　monkeys　　　　　　jumping

Building Vocabulary With Familiar Songs © 2007 by Kathleen Dorsey, Scholastic Teaching Resources

Word Bank

primates

commanded

warned

bounding

skull

miniature

prescribed

tumbled

hurdling

petite

beckoned

plummeted

consulted

bashed

If You're Happy and You Know It

If you're scared and you know it,

Hide your eyes.

If you're scared and you know it,

Hide your eyes.

If you're scared and you know it,

Then your face will surely show it,

If you're scared and you know it,

Hide your eyes.

If you're sad and you know it,
Cry a tear.
If you're sad and you know it,
Cry a tear.
If you're sad and you know it,
Then your face will surely show it,
If you're sad and you know it,
Cry a tear.

If you're angry and you know it,
Stomp your feet.
If you're angry and you know it,
Stomp your feet.
If you're angry and you know it,
Then your face will surely show it,
If you're angry and you know it,
Stomp your feet.

If you're happy and you know it,
Shout "Hurray!"
If you're happy and you know it,
Shout "Hurray!"
If you're happy and you know it,
Then your face will surely show it
If you're happy and you know it,
Shout "Hurray!"

If You're Happy and You Know It

Word Bank

terrified

veil

display

whimper

dejected

weep

miserable

definitely

timorous

exhibit

anxious

visage

conceal

disheartened

certainly

trample

screen

Directions: Fill in the blanks with synonyms from the Word Bank.

If you're _____ and you know it,
                    scared

_____ your eyes.
        Hide

If you're _____ and you know it,
                    scared

_____ your eyes.
        Hide

If you're _____ and you know it,
                    scared

Then your _____ will
                    face

_____   _____ it,
        surely   show

If you're _____ and you know it,
                    scared

_____ your eyes.
        Hide

If you're _____ and you know it,
                    sad

_____ a tear.
        Cry

If you're _____ and you know it,
                    sad

_____ a tear.
        Cry

If you're _____ and you know it,
                    sad

Then your _____ will
                    face

_____   _____ it,
        surely   show

If you're _____ and you know it,
                    sad

_____ a tear.
        Cry

Building Vocabulary With Familiar Songs © 2007 by Kathleen Dorsey, Scholastic Teaching Resources

If you're _____ and you know it,
                    angry

_____ your feet.
        Stomp

If you're _____ and you know it,
                    angry

_____ your feet.
        Stomp

If you're _____ and you know it,
                    angry

Then your _____ will
                    face

_____ _____ it,
        surely   show

If you're _____ and you know it,
                    angry

_____ your feet.
        Stomp

If you're _____ and you know it,
                    happy

_____ "Hurray!"
        Shout

If you're _____ and you know it,
                    happy

_____ "Hurray!"
        Shout

If you're _____ and you know it,
                    happy

Then your _____ will
                    face

_____ _____ it,
        surely   show

If you're _____ and you know it,
                    happy

_____ "Hurray!"
        Shout

Word Bank

bellow

cross

annoyed

ecstatic

exultant

irritated

blissful

countenance

infuriated

scream

jovial

clump

holler

illustrate

vexed

indubitably

Jack and Jill

Jack and Jill went up the hill
To fetch a pail of water.
Jack fell down and broke his crown,
And Jill came tumbling after.

Then up got Jack and said to Jill,
As in his arms he took her,
"Brush off that dirt for you're not hurt,
Let's fetch that pail of water."

So Jack and Jill went up the hill
To fetch the pail of water,
And took it home to Mother dear,
Who thanked her son and daughter.

Building Vocabulary With Familiar Songs © 2007 by Kathleen Dorsey, Scholastic Teaching Resources

Jack and Jill

bucket

traveled

stated

impaired

injured

obtain

faltered

muck

appreciated

proceeded

remarked

fractured

plummeting

transported

mound

sprawling

cherished

commented

stumbled

knoll

grime

wounded

filth

beloved

Directions: Fill in the blanks with synonyms from the Word Bank.

Jack and Jill _____ up the _____
went   hill

To _____ a _____ of water.
fetch   pail

Jack _____ down and _____ his crown,
fell   broke

And Jill came _____ after.
tumbling

Then up got Jack and _____ to Jill,
said

As in his arms he took her,

"Brush off that _____ for you're not _____,
dirt   hurt

Let's _____ that _____ of water."
fetch   pail

So Jack and Jill _____ up the _____
went   hill

To _____ the _____ of water,
fetch   pail

And _____ it home to Mother _____,
took   dear

Who _____ her son and daughter.
thanked

London Bridge

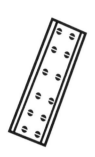

London Bridge is falling down,
Falling down, falling down.
London Bridge is falling down,
My fair lady!

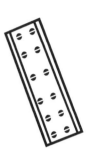

Build it up with iron and steel,
Iron and steel, iron and steel.
Build it up with iron and steel,
My fair lady!

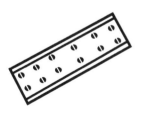

Iron and steel will bend and bow,
Bend and bow, bend and bow.
Iron and steel will bend and bow,
My fair lady!

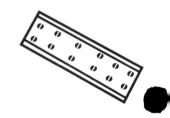

Name _____   Date _____

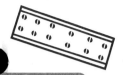

London Bridge

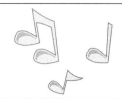

Word Bank

fracture

lovely

construct

just

assemble

manufacture

curve

attractive

flex

plummeting

beautiful

tumbling

arch

toppling

Directions: Fill in the blanks with synonyms from the Word Bank.

London Bridge is _____ down,
falling

_____ down, _____ down.
Falling   falling

London Bridge is _____ down,
falling

My _____ lady!
fair

_____ it up with iron and steel,
Build

Iron and steel, iron and steel.

_____ it up with iron and steel,
Build

My _____ lady!
fair

Iron and steel will _____ and
bend

_____,
bow

_____ and _____,
Bend   bow

_____ and _____.
bend   bow

Iron and steel will _____ and
bend

_____,
bow

My _____ lady!
fair

Mary Had a Little Lamb

Mary had a little lamb,
Little lamb, little lamb,
Mary had a little lamb,
Its fleece was white as snow.

And everywhere that Mary went,
Mary went, Mary went,
Everywhere that Mary went
The lamb was sure to go.

It followed her to school one day,
School one day, school one day.
It followed her to school one day,
Which was against the rule.

It made the children laugh and play,
Laugh and play, laugh and play,
It made the children laugh and play
To see a lamb at school.

Building Vocabulary With Familiar Songs © 2007 by Kathleen Dorsey, Scholastic Teaching Resources

And so the teacher turned it out,
Turned it out, turned it out,
And so the teacher turned it out,
But still it lingered near.

And waited patiently about,
Patiently about, patiently about,
And waited patiently about
Till Mary did appear.

"Why does the lamb love Mary so?
Love Mary so? Love Mary so?
Why does the lamb love Mary so?"
The eager children cry.

"Why, Mary loves the lamb, you know.
Loves the lamb, you know,
Loves the lamb, you know.
Why, Mary loves the lamb, you know."
The teacher did reply.

Mary Had a Little Lamb

Word Bank

glimpse

owned

trailed

chuckle

regulation

possessed

witness

pursued

certain

journeyed

policy

chased

traveled

diminutive

giggle

observe

miniature

chortle

guaranteed

petite

Directions: Fill in the blanks with synonyms from the Word Bank.

Mary _____ a _____ lamb,
          had   little

_____ lamb, _____ lamb,
  Little   little

Mary _____ a _____ lamb,
          had   little

Its fleece was white as snow.

And everywhere that Mary _____,
                          went

Mary _____, Mary _____,
      went   went

Everywhere that Mary _____
                    went

The lamb was _____ to go.
              sure

It _____ her to school one day,
    followed

School one day, school one day.

It _____ her to school one day,
    followed

Which was against the _____.
                   rule

It made the children _____ and play,
                laugh

_____ and play, _____ and play,
  Laugh   laugh

It made the children _____ and play
                laugh

To _____ a lamb at school.
   see

And so the teacher _____ it out,
                          turned

_____ it out, _____ it out,
   Turned   turned

And so the teacher _____ it out,
                          turned

But still it _____ near.
                 lingered

And waited _____ about,
                patiently

_____ about, _____ about,
   Patiently   patiently

And waited _____ about
                patiently

Till Mary did _____.
                   appear

"Why does the lamb _____ Mary so?
                         love

_____ Mary so? _____ Mary so?
   Love   Love

Why does the lamb _____ Mary so?"
                        love

The _____ children _____.
       eager   cry

"Why, Mary _____ the lamb, you know.
                 loves

_____ the lamb, you know,
   Loves

_____ the lamb, you know.
   Loves

Why, Mary _____ the lamb, you know."
                loves

The teacher did _____.
                     reply

Word Bank

adore

enthusiastic

fancy

materialize

exclaim

unwearyingly

excited

respond

keen

ejected

retort

tolerantly

evicted

emerge

loitered

yell

expelled

remained

She'll Be Coming Round the Mountain

She'll be coming round the mountain when she comes.
She'll be coming round the mountain when she comes.
She'll be coming round the mountain,
She'll be coming round the mountain,
She'll be coming round the mountain when she comes.

She'll be driving six white horses when she comes.
She'll be driving six white horses when she comes.
She'll be driving six white horses,
She'll be driving six white horses,
She'll be driving six white horses when she comes.

Oh, we'll all go out to meet her when she comes.
Oh, we'll all go out to meet her when she comes.
Oh, we'll all go out to meet her,
We'll all go out to meet her,
We'll all go out to meet her when she comes.

She'll be wearing red pajamas when she comes.

She'll be wearing red pajamas when she comes.

She'll be wearing red pajamas,

She'll be wearing red pajamas,

She'll be wearing red pajamas when she comes.

She will have to sleep with Grandma when she comes.

She will have to sleep with Grandma when she comes.

She will have to sleep with Grandma,

She will have to sleep with Grandma,

She will have to sleep with Grandma when she comes.

She'll Be Coming Round the Mountain

Directions: Fill in the blanks with synonyms from the Word Bank.

arriving

appears

maneuvering

handling

approaching

join

peak

approaches

directing

welcome

She'll be _____ round the _____
          coming   mountain

when she _____.
          comes

She'll be _____ round the _____
          coming   mountain

when she _____.
          comes

She'll be _____ round the _____,
          coming   mountain

She'll be _____ round the _____,
          coming   mountain

She'll be _____ round the _____
          coming   mountain

when she _____.
          comes

She'll be _____ six white horses when she
          driving

_____.
          comes

She'll be _____ six white horses when she
          driving

_____.
          comes

She'll be _____ six white horses,
          driving

She'll be _____ six white horses,
          driving

She'll be _____ six white horses when she
          driving

_____.
          comes

Oh, we'll all go out to _____ her when she
                         meet

_____.
          comes

Oh, we'll all go out to _____ her when she

meet

_____.

comes

Oh, we'll all go out to _____ her,

meet

We'll all go out to _____ her,

meet

We'll all go out to _____ her when she

meet

_____.

comes

She'll be _____ _____ pajamas

wearing   red

when she _____.

comes

She'll be _____ _____ pajamas

wearing   red

when she _____.

comes

She'll be _____ _____ pajamas,

wearing   red

She'll be _____ _____ pajamas,

wearing   red

She'll be _____ _____ pajamas

wearing   red

when she _____.

comes

She will have to _____ with Grandma when she

sleep

_____.

comes

She will have to _____ with Grandma when she

sleep

_____.

comes

She will have to _____ with Grandma,

sleep

She will have to _____ with Grandma,

sleep

She will have to _____ with Grandma when she

sleep

_____.

comes

Word Bank

scarlet

donning

sporting

ruby

crimson

slumber

snooze

greet

arrives

Six Little Ducks

Six little ducks that I once knew
Fat ones, skinny ones, fair ones, too
But the one little duck with the feather on his back
He led the others with a quack, quack, quack
Quack, quack, quack,
Quack, quack, quack,
He led the others with a quack, quack, quack.

Down to the river they would go
Wibble, wobble, wibble, wobble, to and fro
But the one little duck with the feather on his back
He led the others with a quack, quack, quack,
Quack, quack, quack,
Quack, quack, quack,
He led the others with a quack, quack, quack.

Back from the river they would come
Wibble, wobble, wibble, wobble, ho, hum, hum
But the one little duck with the feather on his back
He led the others with a quack, quack, quack
Quack, quack, quack,
Quack, quack, quack,
He led the others with a quack, quack, quack.

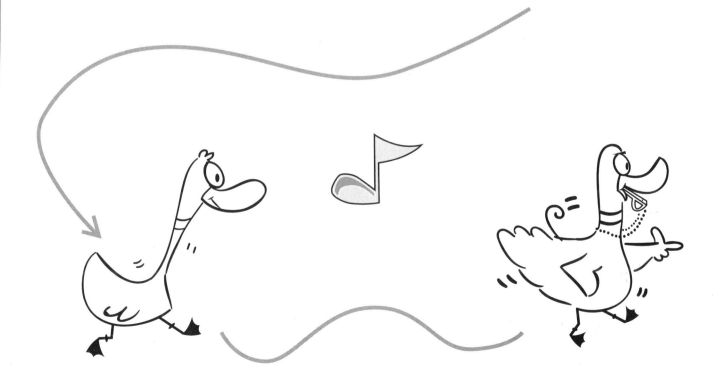

Six Little Ducks

Word Bank

rear
diminutive
directed
plump
corpulent
previously
emaciated
petite
tributary
arrive
formerly
flaxen
pale

Directions: Fill in the blanks with synonyms from the Word Bank.

Six _____ ducks that I _____ knew,
little   once

_____ ones, _____ ones,
Fat   skinny

_____ ones, too
fair

But the one _____ duck with the feather on his
little

_____,
back

He _____ the others with a quack, quack, quack
led

Quack, quack, quack,

Quack, quack, quack,

He _____ the others with a quack, quack, quack.
led

Down to the _____ they would
river

_____,
go

Wibble, wobble, wibble, wobble, to and fro,

But the one _____ duck with the feather on his
little

_____,
back

Building Vocabulary With Familiar Songs © 2007 by Kathleen Dorsey, Scholastic Teaching Resources

He _____ the others with a quack, quack, quack,
         led

Quack, quack, quack,

Quack, quack, quack,

He _____ the others with a quack, quack, quack.
         led

Back from the _____ they would _____,
                    river   come

Wibble, wobble, wibble, wobble, ho, hum, hum,

But the one _____ duck with the feather on his
                  little

_____,
     back

He _____ the others with a quack, quack, quack,
         led

Quack, quack, quack,

Quack, quack, quack,

He _____ the others with a quack, quack, quack.
         led

Word Bank

posterior

approach

stream

lean

piloted

travel

escorted

proceed

canal

slight

stout

hind

scrawny

Baa Baa Black Sheep

Baa baa black sheep
Have you any wool?
Yes sir, yes sir, three bags full!
One for the master,
One for the dame,
And one for the little boy
Who lives down the lane.

Name _____ Date _____

Baa Baa Black Sheep

overflowing   mistress   petite   minute   dwells

landlord   tiny   lad   crammed   path

ebony   resides   youngster   lady   track

Directions: Fill in the blanks with synonyms from the Word Bank.

Baa baa _____ sheep
_{black} below: black

Have you any wool?

Yes sir, yes sir, three bags _____!
full

One for the _____,
master

One for the _____,
dame

And one for the _____ _____
little   boy

Who _____ down the _____.
lives   lane

Little Boy Blue

Little Boy Blue
come blow your horn.
The sheep's in the meadow,
the cow's in the corn.
But where's the boy
who looks after the sheep?
He's under a haystack
fast asleep.
Will you wake him?
No, not I—
for if I do,
he's sure to cry.

Little Boy Blue

Word Bank

slumbering
awaken
youngster
bovine
watches
field
whimper
tends
beneath
rouse
pasture
weep
certain
toot
trumpet
wail
guaranteed
lad
snoozing
bugle
surveys
maize
underneath
blare
observes

Directions: Fill in the blanks with synonyms from the Word Bank.

Little Boy Blue

come _____ your _____ .
                blow   horn

The sheep's in the _____ ,
                            meadow

the _____ 's in the _____ ;
          cow   corn

But where's the _____
                          boy

who _____ after the sheep?
          looks

He's _____ a haystack
            under

fast _____ .
            asleep

Will you _____ him?
                  wake

No, not I—

for if I do,

he's _____ to _____ .
          sure   cry

Little Miss Muffet

Little Miss Muffet sat on a tuffet,
Eating her curds and whey.
Along came a spider,
Who sat down beside her
And frightened Miss Muffet away.

Name _____ Date _____

Little Miss Muffet

startled   arrived   low stool   approached   hassock

consuming   slight   arachnid

alongside   ingesting   alarmed   adjacent to   petite

Directions: Fill in the blanks with synonyms from the Word Bank.

_____ Miss Muffet sat on a _____,
Little   tuffet

_____ her curds and whey.
Eating

Along _____ a _____,
          came   spider

Who sat down _____ her
                    beside

And _____ Miss Muffet away.
        frightened

Old King Cole

Old King Cole
was a merry old soul,
and a merry soul was he;
He called for his pipe
in the middle of the night
and he called for his fiddlers three.
Every fiddler had a fine fiddle,
and a very fine fiddle had he;
Oh there's none so rare
as can compare
With King Cole and his fiddlers three.

Name _____   Date _____

Old King Cole

exceptional

joyous

superior

singular

demanded

aged

first-rate

violin

violinists

elderly

trio

mature

uncommon

cheerful

extremely

summoned

jovial

ordered

incredibly

exceptionally

Directions: Fill in the blanks with synonyms from the Word Bank.

Old King Cole

was a _____ _____ soul,
            merry   old

and a _____ soul was he;
           merry

He _____ for his pipe
        called

in the middle of the night

and he _____ for his _____
           called   fiddlers

_____.
    three

Every _____ had a _____
          fiddler   fine

_____,
    fiddle

and a _____ _____
        very   fine

_____ had he;
    fiddle

Oh there's none so _____
            rare

as can compare

With King Cole and his _____
            fiddlers

_____.
    three

Old Mother Hubbard

Old mother Hubbard
Went to the cupboard
To get her poor doggie a bone.
When she got there
The cupboard was bare
So the poor little doggie had none.

Old Mother Hubbard

Word Bank

elderly   miniature   nil   closet   empty   impoverished   deprived

diminutive

arrived   canine   unfortunate   aged   proceeded   zilch   procure

vacant   obtain   ambled   reached   sauntered   cabinet

Directions: Fill in the blanks with synonyms from the Word Bank.

_____ mother Hubbard
Old

_____ to the _____
Went   cupboard

To _____ her _____ _____ a bone.
get   poor   doggie

When she _____ there
got

The _____ was _____
cupboard   bare

So the _____ _____ _____
poor   little   doggie

had _____.

Twinkle Twinkle Little Star

Twinkle, twinkle, little star,
how I wonder what you are?
Up above the world so high,
like a diamond in the sky.

When the blazing sun is gone,
when he nothing shines upon,
then you show your little light,
twinkle, twinkle all the night.

Then the traveler in the dark
thanks you for your tiny spark,
he could not see which way to go
if you did not twinkle so.

In the dark blue sky you keep,
and often through my curtains peep,
for you never shut your eye,
'till the sun is in the sky.

As your bright and tiny spark
lights the traveler in the dark,
though I know not what you are,
twinkle, twinkle, little star.

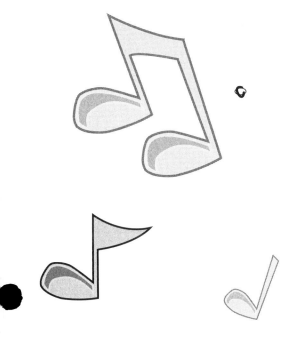

☆Twinkle Twinkle Little Star

Word Bank

beams

atmosphere

minute

slight

radiating

shadows

dusk

sparkle

question

elevated

appreciates

lofty

speculate

radiates

scorching

cherishes

Directions: Fill in the blanks with synonyms from the Word Bank.

_____, _____, _____ star,
Twinkle   twinkle   little

how I _____ what you are?
wonder

Up above the world so _____,
high

like a diamond in the _____.
sky

When the _____ sun is gone,
blazing

when he nothing _____ upon,
shines

then you show your _____ light,
little

_____, _____ all the night.
twinkle   twinkle

Then the traveler in the _____
dark

_____ you for your tiny spark,
thanks

he could not see which way to go

if you did not _____ so.
twinkle

Building Vocabulary With Familiar Songs © 2007 by Kathleen Dorsey, Scholastic Teaching Resources

In the dark _____ _____ you keep,
   blue   sky

and often through my _____ _____,
                        curtains   peep

for you never shut your eye,

'till the sun is in the _____.
                         sky

As your _____ and tiny spark
          bright

lights the traveler in the _____,
                              dark

though I know not what you are,

_____, _____,
   twinkle   twinkle

_____ star.
   little

glance

dimness

azure

shades

gloom

vivid

dazzling

cobalt

shutters

drapes

sapphire

glimmer

firmament

peek

Hey Diddle Diddle

Hey diddle, diddle,
The cat and the fiddle,
The cow jumped over the moon.
The little dog laughed
To see such fun
And the dish ran away with the spoon!

Hey Diddle Diddle

Word Bank

giggled   violin   bovine   canine   feline   behold

plate   scampered   platter   chuckled   merriment   leaped

witness   observe   hurdled   scurried   soared   hilarity

Directions: Fill in the blanks with synonyms from the Word Bank.

Hey diddle, diddle,

The _____ and the _____,
    cat   fiddle

The _____ _____ over the moon.
    cow   jumped

The little _____ _____
          dog   laughed

To _____ such _____
   see   fun

And the _____ _____ away with the spoon!
        dish   ran

Simple Simon

Simple Simon met a pie man
Going to the fair;
Says Simple Simon to the pie man,
"Let me try your ware."

Said the pie man to Simple Simon,
"Show me first your penny."
Said Simple Simon to the pie man,
"Sir, I have not any."

Simple Simon

Directions: Fill in the blanks with synonyms from the Word Bank.

Word Bank

remarks

departing

approached

utters

festival

goods

answered

responded

merchandise

fete

setting off

carnival

sample

reveal

replied

encountered

nibble

confronted

display

Simple Simon _____ a pie man
                          met

_____ to the _____;
          Going   fair

_____ Simple Simon to the pie man,
          Says

"Let me _____ your _____."
                  try   ware

_____ the pie man to Simple Simon,
          Said

" _____ me first your penny."
          Show

_____ Simple Simon to the pie man,
          Said

" Sir, I have not any."

Answer Key

Be Kind to Your Web-Footed Friends (p. 7)
kind – benevolent, compassionate, considerate;
friends – acquaintances, associates, comrades;
swamp – bog, marsh, morass; **weather** – climate;
damp – clammy, moist, humid; **think** – assume,
believe, imagine; **end** – conclusion, finale

In a Cabin in the Woods (p. 9)
cabin – cottage, bungalow, lodge; **little** –
diminutive, miniature, petite; **old** – elderly, mature;
saw – observed, watched; **hopping** – bounding,
skipping; **knocking** – thumping, tapping, rapping;
door – entrance; **help** – aid, assist; **said** – pleaded,
begged; **safely** – securely; **abide** – dwell, reside

Do Your Ears Hang Low? (pp. 12–13)
hang – dangle, droop, drape; **wobble** – vibrate,
quiver, tremble; **tie** – bind, fasten; **throw** – fling,
pitch; **sky** – atmosphere, firmament; **wrinkle**
– crumple, crease, rumple; **wet** – sodden, moist,
soppy; **dry** – desiccated, parched, dehydrated;
wave – brandish, undulate; **flap** – flutter, flail;
breeze – gust, draft; **little** – miniature, minute; **soar**
– escalate, ascend; **nation** – country, homeland,
realm; **feeling** – sensation; **big** – enormous,
immense, gigantic; **lie** – recline; **bounce** – rebound,
spring; **sound** – resonance, reverberation; **stick**
– deposit, plunk

Itsy Bitsy Spider (p. 15)
itsy bitsy – diminutive, minuscule, minute; **spider** –
arachnid; **climbed** – clambered, ascended, mounted,
scaled; **rain** – precipitation, drizzle; **washed**
– swept, inundated; **dried up** – evaporated

The Farmer in the Dell (pp. 18–19)
dell – glade, hollow; **takes** – procures, obtains,
acquires; **wife** – spouse, partner; **child** – descendant,
offspring; **nurse** – nanny, baby-sitter; **cow**
– bovine; **dog** – canine; **cat** – feline; **rat** – rodent;
stands – exists, persists, endures; **alone** – solitary,
unaccompanied, forlorn

Five Little Monkeys (pp. 22–23)
little – diminutive, petite, miniature; **monkeys**
– primates; **jumping** – leaping, bounding, vaulting,
hurdling; **fell** – tumbled, plummeted; **bumped** –

smacked, walloped, bashed; **head** – skull, cranium
called – summoned, beckoned, consulted; **doctor**
– medic, physician; **said** – instructed, ordered,
commanded, warned, prescribed

If You're Happy and You Know It (pp. 26–27)
scared – terrified, timorous, anxious; **hide**
– conceal, screen, veil; **face** – visage, countenance;
surely – indubitably, certainly, definitely; **show**
– display, illustrate, exhibit; **sad** – miserable,
dejected, disheartened; **cry** – weep, whimper; **angry**
– annoyed, irritated, infuriated, cross, vexed; **stomp**
– clump, trample; **happy** – blissful, jovial, ecstatic,
exultant; **shout** – scream, bellow, holler

Jack and Jill (p. 29)
went – traveled, proceeded; **hill** – mound, knoll;
fetch – obtain; **pail** – bucket; **fell** – faltered,
stumbled; **broke** – impaired, fractured; **tumbling**
– plummeting, sprawling; **said** – stated, commented,
remarked; **dirt** – muck, grime, filth; **hurt** – injured,
wounded; **took** – transported; **dear** – cherished,
beloved; **thanked** – appreciated

London Bridge (p. 31)
falling – toppling, plummeting, tumbling; **fair**
– lovely, attractive, beautiful, just; **build** – construct,
assemble, manufacture; **bend** – flex, arch; **bow**
– curve, fracture

Mary Had a Little Lamb (pp. 34–35)
had – possessed, owned; **little** – petite, diminutive,
miniature; **went** – journeyed, traveled; **sure**
– guaranteed, certain; **followed** – pursued, chased,
trailed; **rule** – regulation, policy; **laugh** – chuckle,
giggle, chortle; **see** – glimpse, witness, observe;
turned – expelled, evicted, ejected; **lingered**
– loitered, remained; **patiently** – unwearyingly,
tolerantly; **appear** – materialize, emerge; **love/loves**
– adore, fancy; **eager** – enthusiastic, excited, keen;
cry – exclaim, yell; **reply** – respond, retort

She'll Be Coming Round the Mountain
(pp. 38–39)
coming – arriving, approaching; **mountain** – peak;
comes – appears, arrives, approaches; **driving**
– maneuvering, handling, directing; **meet** – join,

Building Vocabulary With Familiar Songs © 2007 by Kathleen Dorsey, Scholastic Teaching Resources

welcome, greet; **wearing** – donning, sporting; **red** – scarlet, ruby, crimson; **sleep** – snooze, slumber

Six Little Ducks (pp. 42–43)
little – diminutive, petite; **once** – previously, formerly; **fat** – plump, corpulent, stout; **skinny** – emaciated, lean, scrawny, slight; **fair** – flaxen, pale; **back** – rear, posterior, hind; **led** – directed, piloted, escorted; **river** – tributary, stream, canal; **go** – travel, proceed; **come** – arrive, approach

Baa Baa Black Sheep (p. 45)
black – ebony; **full** – overflowing, crammed; **master** – landlord; **dame** – mistress, lady; **little** – petite, minute, tiny; **boy** – lad, youngster; **lives** – dwells, resides; **lane** – path, track

Little Boy Blue (p. 47)
blow – blare, toot; **horn** – trumpet, bugle; **meadow** – field, pasture; **cow** – bovine; **corn** – maize; **boy** – youngster, lad; **looks** – watches, surveys, observes, tends; **under** – underneath, beneath; **asleep** – slumbering, snoozing; **wake** – awaken, rouse; **sure** – guaranteed, certain; **cry** – wail, weep, whimper

Little Miss Muffet (p. 49)
little – petite, slight; **tuffet** – low stool, hassock; **eating** – ingesting, consuming; **came** – arrived, approached; **spider** – arachnid; **beside** – alongside, adjacent to; **frightened** – startled, alarmed

Old King Cole (p. 51)
merry – joyous, cheerful, jovial; **old** – elderly, mature, aged; **called** – demanded, summoned, ordered; **fiddler(s)** – violinists; **three** – trio; **fine** – exceptional, superior, first-rate; **fiddle** – violin; **very** – exceptionally, extremely, incredibly; **rare** – uncommon, singular

Old Mother Hubbard (p. 53)
old – elderly, aged; **went** – ambled, sauntered, proceeded; **cupboard** – closet, cabinet; **get** – obtain, procure; **poor** – impoverished, deprived, unfortunate; **doggie** – canine; **got** – arrived, reached; **bare** – vacant, empty; **little** – miniature, diminutive; **none** – zilch, nil

Twinkle Twinkle Little Star (pp. 56–57)
twinkle – sparkle, glimmer; **little** – minute, slight; **wonder** – speculate, question; **high** – elevated, lofty; **sky** – firmament, atmosphere; **blazing** – radiating, scorching; **shines** – radiates, beams; **dark** – dimness, dusk, shadows, gloom; **thanks** – appreciates, cherishes; **blue** – azure, sapphire, cobalt; **curtains** – shutters, drapes, shades; **peep** – peek, glance; **bright** – vivid, dazzling

Hey Diddle Diddle (p. 59)
cat – feline; **fiddle** – violin; **cow** – bovine; **jumped** – hurdled, soared, leaped; **dog** – canine; **laughed** – giggled, chuckled; **see** – behold, witness, observe; **fun** – merriment, hilarity; **dish** – plate, platter; **ran** – scampered, scurried

Simple Simon (p. 61)
met – approached, encountered, confronted; **going** – departing, setting off; **fair** – festival, fete, carnival; **says** – remarks, utters; **try** – sample, nibble; **ware** – goods, merchandise; **said** – answered, responded, replied; **show** – reveal, display

Bibliography

Christen, W. L., & Murphy, T. J. (1991). Increasing comprehension by activating prior knowledge. *ERIC Digest*. Bloomington, IN: ERIC Clearinghouse on Reading, English, and Communication

McKeown, M. G., & Beck, I. L. (1998). Learning vocabulary: Different ways for different goals. *Remedial and Special Education (RASE), 9(1),* 42–46.

Nagy, W. E., et al (1985). Learning word meanings from context: How broadly generalizable? Technical Report No. 347. Urbana, IL: Center for the Study of Reading

Nagy, W. E. (1988). *Teaching Vocabulary to Improve Reading Comprehension*. Urbana, IL: National Council of Teachers of English; Newark, DE: International Reading Association [ED 298 471]

Swanborn, M. S. L., & de Glopper, K. (1999). Incidental word learning while reading: A meta-analysis. *Review of Educational Research, 69(3),* pp. 261–285

Wilkinson, M. (1994). Using student stories to build vocabulary in cooperative learning groups. *Clearing House, 67(4),* 221–23.